The Grandmother Poems

Marcia Katz Wolf

Plain View Press
P. O. 42255
Austin, TX 78704

plainviewpress.net
sb@plainviewpress.net
512-441-2452

Copyright Marcia Katz Wolf 2009. All rights reserved.
ISBN: 978-1-935514-51-0
Library of Congress Number: 2009929325

Cover art by Lynn Mauser-Bain
Cover design by Susan Bright

For Al Jacobs (1937-2008)
a beloved friend and this book's midwife

Contents

Summer

Folding Clothes While My Granddaughter Sleeps	9
If Voices	10
Claire	11
For Genny Calderon	12
To Be	14
Driving Home	15
For Josh	16
The Mind/Body Problem	17
A Jew Walking On a Sunday	18
Mika	19
The New Love	20
Swinging – Post Robert Louis Stevenson	21
Sunday, Sunday	22
After Babysitting	23

Autumn

I Saw It At the Movies	27
Walking My Granddaughter To School	29
Housekeeping	30
Yonatan	31
At the End Of World War II	32
Numbering	33
My Mother's Story	34
Vacuuming	35
No	36
Drinking Lattes	37
In the Evening	38
Outside	39
The Food Bank	40
The Hair Cut	41
Gentle Annie	43
Fall	44

Winter

Christmas, 1947	47
According To the LA Times	50
1976	51
1942	51
If I Hate My Husband	52
Provisioning	53
If the Universe	54
The Solipsism Of the Suicide's Child	55
For Primo Levi	56
Steal Away	57
At the Light	58
Singing With Jennie	59
Birthday Card	60
On Memory	61

Spring

Letter From London In 1958 When I Was Sixteen	65
Joseph Le Conte Junior High School	67
The Chemistry Of Love	72
At the Bank With Claire 30 Years Ago	73
A True Story	74
Philip	75
Reading Borges	76
Violation	77
Karen	78
Yeats Changes His Itinerary	79
"Joe Hill"	80

Notes	82
About the Author	83

Summer

Folding Clothes While My Granddaughter Sleeps

Folding clothes on my daughter's bed where Mika lies napping,
piles of socks and shirts and pants enclosing her dreams
until there is no more room and I say to Emily,
"Your children have too many clothes,"
and she says, "I don't want them not to have choices"—
then I see towers rising higher and higher
of all the garments Mika will wear
to all the places she will go, and turn away from,
wearing and discarding, for love, for work,
for babies, for grief.
Watching her here in her fabric stronghold, I make a wish
that in years and years from now
as she folds clothes around her grandchild's dreams,
she too will find release in this baby's sweet sleep, still
heedless of the frays
heedless of the tears.

If Voices

If voices traveled like the light of stars long dead,
where is my grandmother saying still:
"Look, Anne, she drank all her borscht
and ate every morsel of smoked fish, *kine hora*."
Or my mother's, "Ah, Marcia,
to know that life is tragic
is the beginning of wisdom— read
Chekov's *The Lady with the Pet Dog*.
Or the voice of my father behind me
as I walk through the living room, doorbell ringing
on the night of my senior prom:
"Your nylons— the seams are crooked—fix them."
And just as I'm about to open the door—
"If I had met someone who looked like you when I was 17,
I would have fallen in love with her."

Claire

Claire, my lamb
my sea-star, my fish
you go on sea legs still
uncertain as the wind
turns your fur back
on pale skin
feathers trembling like dandelions
in late summer—
why can't you see
the light on your back,
glittering scales dancing?
It cannot be borne
the twiggy legs and
ribs of straw
tender buds of kidneys
footpads of pink foam
and the courage unknowable
as just before the spark
that flared into time—

I would bring you antlers of rock
and hooves of stone
skin of hammered kryptonite
lungs of the baleen, its submarine sense
trunks of the redwood
to root you for a thousand years
   so you would never drown   ,   ever

      find
          ease in water
              tail flashing beneath your belly
in the sun.

For Genny Calderon

Yesterday after my mammogram
(why do I think now 'picture of mother'?)
the technician tells me, "The images are clear/you can go.
If anything shows up, we'll call."
As I stand, a woman across from me in a faded blue hospital gown,
hand across one breast, says, "I had to come back.
They called—I'm so scared."
Even knowing I'm failing her, I say, "Try to relax, breathe deep—
nine times out of ten, everything's fine...they're just careful here,"
her eyes so wide open, both arms across her chest now.
"Shall I keep you company while you wait?" I ask.
"Please."
We talk of her life in Peru and Chile
of her home in the mountains of Cuzco, her condo in Sunnyvale,
my daughter's apartment in Mountain View,
of taxes and interest rates, profits and capital gains,
of how every morning before she goes to work
she walks in the woods near her house—
of the trees and the air,
her mother's death at 56 from breast cancer,
her grandfather, the President of Peru in 1942 (my birth year),
of her brother, a senator there now, of my children
and grandchildren—
that having no one here she will return to Peru, she says,
when this is all over,
when just then a technician appears,
holds two thumbs up: "All clear. You can go home."
We stand and cheer and cry and hold each other a long time—
"Come to my house," she says, "you and your husband,
I'll make you paella before I go back to my country."
"We'll be there," I say, and I give her my number,

12

but even if she never calls,
I will always know
that I came upon without warning
in the basement of Kaiser Hospital
in the Department of Mammography
perfect love.

To Be

Hand in hand with Mika along the corridor of her nursery school,
she stops, pivots, caught by something at her eye level—
takes a breath, holds it, exhales and whispers,
"Oh wow— 2P"—
in front of her, hanging on a peg,
a child's glossy pink plastic backpack
embossed with three Disney figures:
Cinderella, Belle, and Snow White—
"2 P?" I ask,
she points to the figures,
I think to myself, 'She counts, *one…two…p*, unable to say *th*'—
"Oh, very good, Mika— one, two, three princesses."
"No, Damma. 2P."
"P for princess?"
She searches my face, then turns,
and we continue on our way, she in her world
me in mine
until we open her front door
where on the threshold
her babysitter, Filippa, hands her a pair of shoes,
pink with pink star-shaped sequins— and at each sparkly toe
grinning saucily from a white plastic cloud,
Ariel, Belle, and Cinderella—
"Oh, Fee-pa— 2P!"
Just what Hamlet must have said
when he first saw Ophelia playing in the castle garden
(and, what a shame, that later
things had to change)
                      Please, God,
grant Mika's parents all the therapy they will ever need
so that her perfect poem
will never not be
"Oh wow— 2P!"

Driving Home

After visiting relatives in Santa Barbara, and a childhood friend,
at the beginning of my drive back to northern California,
I saw again the sign marking an exit my mother took for 30 years
to get home: La Cumbra/Hope—
and felt the old, 'how can it be that she is gone?'
when just then a song on my Stephen Foster tape began,
"Let us pause in life's pleasures and count every tear
while we all.................sorrow."
What was the word after *all*? Was it *sop* or *sob*, or *salve*?
I turned up the volume and rewound, but still could not get it,
so, taking my life in my hands as I drove the 101,
I rewound and played, rewound again—
But it was impossible to make out
just what it was we were to do with sorrow.
On television that night, a former teacher of mine,
speaking of the great Polish poet, Czeslaw Milosz, now dead,
said he had lost so much, that is why he wrote poetry, perhaps,
to preserve what he had left—
and though what I have lost is not much more or less than most,
a mother, father, step-son, some friends—
I think now, having listened to my old professor,
the hardest thing, there is no teaching for,
what to do with sorrow—
as I sit in my living room,
trying to write this poem,
300 miles past the La Cumbra/Hope exit,
on the way to where my mother once lived.

For Josh

Twenty-five years after my step-son was killed
in a helicopter crash in Alaska
on his way from the small island Petersburgh to the mainland,
two weeks after his twenty-first birthday,
I cannot watch our daughter back her car out of the driveway,
red Geo disappearing around the corner—
"If she's going to drive the freeway,
she needs a bigger car," I say to my husband.
"Small cars are more maneuverable."
"For you," I say.
"A big car is not safer," that engineer tone.
"You've lost one child," I say calmly,
"Isn't that enough?"
He says nothing
and then again nothing—
Where desperate love is, cruelty
will not be far behind.

The Mind/Body Problem

"Why ever did you do that?"

he asked,

as if I held

the answer he sought—

as if thought were the

lever of doing,

My body, the brain's

marionette . But

This Doll

is devilishly clever,

& answers us only

with sighs.

A Jew Walking On a Sunday

Last Sunday morning as I was taking a walk,
I passed a cop sitting in his car
at the corner of California Avenue and Park Street,
tanned arm resting on the window ledge,
big silver watch he was checking–
I smiled as I caught his eye
and he smiled back– sadly, I thought,
as if to say, "Here it is Sunday morning,
and I'm all alone in a police vehicle,"
trigger hand splayed across the steering wheel–
I thought to brush its flurry of soft hair,
say, "Turn on your radio to 88.5 fm,
there's usually gospel music on about now"–
but because I was afraid
and genes will out
I withheld my succor
and kept on wandering–

Mika

On a day when everything is a poem,
I'm at an outdoor cafe with my granddaughter
who's plunging four plump fingers
into a small tub of cream cheese,
scooping it into her mouth,
utterly absorbed in her sucking,
in the complete fulfillment of desire
and her grandmother beside her,
shoulders rising dimly,
a distant mountain range above the deep basin of her pleasure—
when shimmering in the late morning light
a silver-domed conveyance glides to a gentle stop before us
and, like a photograph developing,
a mysterious stranger materializes,
arms extending in our direction—
when suddenly a car door jerks open,
tree-trunk leg hits the ground
bearing a large belly, thick arms
beefy neck and head—
and I laugh and Mika laughs
and I laugh again
in thankfulness for the perfect joy of my granddaughter
bewitching a dusty gray Datsun
into a radiant, floating carriage—
an unshaven bald guy into Tristan
and grandmother in advanced middle age
into Isolde,
on a very good day
in deed.

The New Love

There is a humming that begins inside
when a poem starts to come round—
it is like falling in love,
the stirring of destiny, time and space opening,
as you become what you behold—
        But sooner or later, a false note
and you're no longer in sync— though for a time,
you count yourself lucky to have something, at least—
When, without warning, a fury sparks,
as in 'he's resisting me,'
cooling into disappointment, as in
'he's unable to become who I thought he could be'—
then the disintegration, 'he was never really who I thought he was,'
and the drifting—
though not so far away
as to be not still vaguely familiar,
still, vaguely, at times, a friend
whose company will, on occasion, suffice
during the long wait
for the rhapsody
of what has not yet
found its tune.

Swinging — Post Robert Louis Stevenson

At the park with Mika, swinging beside her friend, Amy,

her mother pushing her and talking on a cell phone—

"Push me hard, Grandma!"

I try my best—

"I'm going so high," she says

"I'm going higher," Amy says

I push harder—

"I'm high too," Mika

"I'm higher," Amy

Taking a long step, I thrust Mika into the sky,

as the frame shakes and shudders,

and she gasps, laughs and sings out from the summit:

"We're both higher!"

Sunday, Sunday

Could there ever be a better day

than waking this morning to my mind's chanting,

'The man plunges his hands into the chime of the morning'?

In the afternoon Claire singing Handel,

"O Sleep, why dost thou leave me?"

32nd notes, humming birds—

and tonight my husband makes our bed so carefully,

green pillows precisely

where our heads will be,

Euclid whispering,

    sleep
    sleep
    sleep.

After Babysitting

Taking the long way home

   after tending my grandchildren

         (as any good Wolf should do),

the light turned green   &   a   huge   bus

    circled a lovely turn

        in front of me,

sweeping me into its wake ,   the poem

                all day

   I had been waiting for.

Autumn

I Saw It At the Movies

I never liked Dorothy one bit
that plaintive, nasal voice—
and while it is all the rage now
not to see her side of it,
I assert a prior claim
back to half a century ago
at the Lagoon Theatre on Nicollet Avenue
in Minneapolis— it was a Sunday afternoon,
my neighbor Linda Lewis, who played with me
only when there was no one else around,
sitting on my right side and her mother on my left,
Mrs. Lewis who, some years later, would push
at my toilet paper bosom, it rustling
as she prodded, and grill me:
"Is that all you?"
And in spite of her kneading
and their whispered protestations (though she herself hid,
I knew because I saw it,
one rubber bust replacing her
lost, malignant one),
I would not, though torn between shame and fury,
give in to her probings, insisting,
"It's all me, all me"—
because when a few years earlier
in a blast of electrified light
the witch appeared, her huge and poisonous face
I hadn't known until then was mine—
although she would fly from her crimes,
autonomous as air,
and even when cornered at the end,
melted away,
I had to stay behind, knowing
the one thing I could never alter—

continued...

forever hanging on that towering screen—
my green-tinged reflection,
willing to do anything to keep Dorothy away from Kansas
where then she would always be right
around the corner.

Walking My Granddaughter To School

Walking Mika to school this morning,

two young mothers in front of me talking—

"My mother cut off all my hair,"

pointing, as if to a wound, "from here to here,"

as if a knife blade had pierced her hip

and then her neck. "'They're just dead cells,'

my mother said, because that's what mothers say."

Then her friend said what friends say,

"It happened to me too

and I cried and cried."

Housekeeping

Coffee sloshed on the kitchen counter at 5 a.m.,
leaking into silverware drawers,
trickling down cupboards
onto the floor—
instead of taking the slimy floor sponge
my husband keeps under the sink for such occasions,
I unroll 8 lengths of paper towel—
the competent, well groomed,
completely-in-charge, sleek haired lady
in the television commercial
who, tripping like Cyd Charisse,
serving tray sailing in the air,
catches one, two, three delectable items
she then presents to her guests—
   but, this is a lie—
the truth I didn't say,
what I really felt, dabbing the counter dry,
is that I was a young mother again,
patting away the milk
on Emily's bright face.

Yonatan

I had forgotten the word *agony*
until yesterday, its letters appearing
one by one vertically
as I was filling in the horizontal spaces
of the Times crossword—
I had often said *grief, hard times,*
suffering, and *sorrow*
but not, for many years, *agony*
as in "That must be agony for you,
the way he died"—
or, perhaps, lived.
But last night I dreamed that my grandson vanished—
and I searched and searched,
howling to anyone who would stop
of what I had lost—
And now that it is day again,
having recovered agony,
I see that Yonatan
will never completely
be found again.

At the End Of World War II

At the end of World War II when I was three
my mother and I took the overnight train
from St. Paul to Chicago to have her nose done
before my father, a captain in a medical unit returned from France,
the scooped-out flesh, a surprise for him (though, I suppose, he had
grown used to such things).
The story my mother told is that as she lay sleeping
I clambered into her berth and gently removed all the bobby pins
from her straight dark hair "so she looked like a fright
when she went under the knife."
I don't remember the train ride
or how long she was gone
or who took care of me then,
only standing on a street corner, so cold,
looking up at a tall brown building
with black windows— like blind eyes,
like the man who sharpened my grandmother's knives
and spat pink-tinged saliva onto the sidewalk in front of her house
and my mother, shadowed, coming toward me from a long way off,
then, as she neared, a large bandage where her nose had been
and seeing in my mind Queen Celeste with her trunk cut off.
My mother always said she liked her new nose,
pleased by my father's pleasure—
"the doctor, a real artist, he didn't overdo,
just corrected where nature went wrong,"
unlike the drowsy foothills of the Sierras
from which, as I dream, I leap into flight,
and lean my cheek against, whenever we drive northeast
from my new home in Palo Alto.

Numbering

It all started to go down hill
when we began to count— if there were two or three or more
and we had one,
then there must be something missing—
Big and small are okay, necessary even
when it comes to feeding the family
to distinguish between a lion
and a mountain lion—
But there was hell to pay
when my granddaughter learned to count to two
because then one M&M, one cookie, one balloon
would not suffice—
just as standing in this field of late summer poppies
I reckon the months until my next birthday,
afternoon light thinning,
earth tilting toward winter
and I wonder, did the gods invent numbers
or numbers, the gods?
standing here among the poppies
singing to myself, "Wish I were a red rosy bush,"
trying to see the field whole
trying my best
not to count.

My Mother's Story

One day my mother told me that when she was young
she wrote a story about a country where as people got richer
they would cut off a digit of their finger,
replacing it with a porcelain one
embedded with precious and semi-precious stones,
until the very richest no longer had fingers of sinew and bone,
and, so, unable to raise their hands,
they would sit in their tall thrones,
arms held aloft by servants,
hands glinting in the flicker of sconces,
blinding all who passed by.
"I wrote many other stories," she said,
"but never published one word."
In that moment I both entered her and sped light years away—
too close and too far away to embrace her.

Taking a break from writing this poem nearly half a century later,
my mother long dead,
I walk through the dining room on the soft red oriental rug
I paid too much for—
when in the mirror above the Eastlake chest she insisted I buy,
through the lipstick and mascara and blush,
another face beckons—
and again, I am too far away
and much too close
for comfort.

Vacuuming

Irving says to me, "I left the vacuum downstairs
in case there's something you see that I didn't do."

Irving left—

the vacuum

down   stares,

encased—

There's something, you see,

I didn't

do.

No

I will not go

outside again.

Don't show me

one more bright flower.

I cannot forgive it— anything

that does not suffer.

Want no truck

with my girlhood,

its beauty's

sweet trance.

Drinking Lattes

Drinking decaf lattes with two old friends
who haven't seen each other since high school,
the three of us, handsome women still— tart and smart—
Feeling cheered for almost the first time this fall,
I think: if Eve and Manuela and I
spent the rest of our lives together,
shopping, cooking, movies, opera—
then I think I would bear it,
if when death came,
we three lay side by side, holding hands
as we used to— walking down Hollywood Boulevard,
trying on expensive shoes at Mandel's,
falsies and padded girdles at Frederick's,
shoplifting Powder Pink lipstick at the Broadway—
comforted by shared memories—
of Eve's first love, Lornie Newman,
Manuela's mother playing the violin
in that dark, dark house,
of my handsome father
alive then still, for a little longer.
   But what if swept into my own storm of dying
I no longer care that Eve's parents held hands
and sang, "What'll I do when you are far away,
so far away, what'll I do?"—
What if it is not the dying
who can any longer remember and witness,
but only the living
who can wait
and watch?

In the Evening

I walked out one evening

soundlessly,

eyes closed to

what was

recognizable,

lowered

in slow motion

to shadows, the stain

of

no thing—

Outside

Outside the door of my granddaughter's classroom
a young woman with hair still damp
holding her daughter's hand, Starbuck's coffee in the other,
next to her an older man, kind face,
leans toward her and says, "I'll take her in."
He returns shortly, gestures good-bye, and starts toward the exit—
then turns back to her:
"Finish your coffee, Rachel"—
"Is that your father?" I ask.
"No, my friend's father."
"Oh— it was such a father thing to say."
She nods without expression,
and I feel with her—
though Mika greeted me this morning with her radiant face,
arms outstretched,
I fed her breakfast and walked her to school,
picked her up and brushed her off when she tripped—
that it's only other people's fathers who say,
"Finish your coffee, Rachel."

The Food Bank

There is a man who comes regularly
to the food bank where I volunteer,
well-groomed and heartbreakingly handsome—
he reads the sign in front of him:
1 item per shelf
3 servings of produce
2 of the following: eggs, yogurt, margarine
and greets me with a sweet, open smile.
I have a name tag,
but do not ask his name,
saying, for example,
"Hi Ted"—
for then I would know him
and owe him something
I could not give, except this poem
counterfeit tender
with which I pay my debt.

The Hair Cut

In the last week of my mother's life,
she held a newspaper in trembling hands all day long,
rotating it from time to time, a quarter turn,
then staring at it again for a long time,
and then another turn—
Toward dusk on one of these afternoons, she looked up at me,
speaking slowly as gradually she recognized me:
"My father woke every morning before it was light
and fed the furnace to warm the house before he left for work,
yet I can remember only two conversations
I ever had with him"—
as if the newspaper were reading her life to her,
and she translating for me.
Then one or two afternoons before she died,
the same newspaper shaking so,
she put it down and reached out one hand to me,
brushing my jaw with her finger tips—
"Let me trim your hair."
"Why, Mom?"
Here it was— the showdown I'd been dreading
for over a half-century: my mother or my life,
just exactly what my shiny hair
(albeit now artfully darkened) had always been to me.
She must have seen the tic of fear because she added,
"Only a tiny bit, just at the ends— go— get me the scissors."
Then the abyss. Then the leap—
"Okay, Mom."
Eyes focussed, mouth firm, hands steadier now,
she cut a few strands at a time,
tiny pieces floating down to my shoulders and breast—
Finally: "Go. Look."

continued......

In her bathroom mirror, I saw that she had curved the edges
of my fashionable bob,
having taken off no more than a fraction of an inch,
rounding it to the way it was in pictures on my dresser
when I was five or six—
and, so, right before she died,
my mother made me young again,
saw me meek and gentle as a child,
perhaps for the last time.

Gentle Annie

On Saturday, Dec. 7, 1963,
22 years after Pearl Harbor exactly,
my father awoke from his dream of self-slaughter
to almost a new world,
relieved he was not the Yale Katz of the night,
that his wife and children slept still—
that the grassy knoll was just a nightmare,
as was his despair,
and the blood on his breast—
Yet near him all that day, it seemed
someone he once loved, perhaps,
or had he dreamed the hazel eyes and Slavic bones,
dark hair caught high on her head,
who read him Yeats and held his hand,
and walked with him as he wept.
But as the light of that Sabbath fell into dusk,
he felt her turn from him and knew,
that even as he slept,
her pilgrim soul would come to him
no more again.

Fall

It is the fall now
when my husband and I walk
in the late afternoon—
people smile at us passing,
reassured, briefly, that you can be attractive,
and affectionate,
though no longer young,
no longer, even, middle aged—
he, silver haired, tall body just slightly bent,
me, too, and thicker through the middle—
but our shadows are long and straight still—
I keep my eyes on them, the slender arms
and angular shoulders, connected,
without feet or footsteps, we glide as in memory,
except then we danced into the night—
now, as we float and grow toward darkness,
my husband and I and the sun,
we all go in together.

Winter

Christmas, 1947

1.

I never remembered calling my father anything but Dad
until I saw his inscription on the title page of the Golden Bible
I found wedged and crumbling next to the Passover Haggadahs
I was taking out last Sunday,
the writing looping, rhythmic,
"To Marcia and Daniel
Christmas 1947
Love, Daddy"
"My God," I say to my husband, "read this."
"So," as he finishes, "who's Christina?"
"Not Christina," I say, "Christmas."
"He gave you and Dan a Golden Bible for Christmas?"
"Therein lies the tale of the *meshuggah* Katzes," I tell him,
Hebrew name, Cohane Tzadik, *wise priest*,
descended from Aaron, Moses' brother,
my father explained to me years later,
Mother laughing at the Katz pretension,
"Horse thieves, every last one."

2.

Christmas Eve, 1947,
fir tree bare in the corner, my mother at the sink
pouring water into a huge kettle filled with Tide granules,
then heaving it onto the dining room table
where she pushed and prodded the heavy mass,
bending further and further, her face flushed from the labor—
me next to her on a stool rigid in the desperation of waiting,
Dan and the baby asleep upstairs,
as she stirred and beat and whipped it into life,
then touching the rough wooden spoon to the tip of each branch
suddenly, right before my eyes,
the tree bloomed a lacy froth of snow.

continued...

3.

December, 1946, my father home from Europe
less than a year, with a cough and despair,
contracted, both, in the medical unit he served with in France,
"right behind the front lines," my mother told me
after he died 17 years later.
Then he could be heard from upstairs,
coughing in my grandmother's dark basement,
day after day developing photographs, "of the war," he told me,
as I watched his reddish form from the safety of the stairs,
hands rising ghostly from the developing fluid,
retrieving something I could not see.

4.

I never stopped watching him in all the years that followed
until one day not long before my high school graduation,
me standing on the threshold of his study,
he reading a medical journal as I look from him to the bookshelf
at titles that come back to me now almost 50 years later—
Black Lamb and Grey Falcon
The Hebrew Bible
Gargantua and Pentagruel
Gray's Anatomy
The Seven Storey Mountain
Memoirs of Hecate County
and James's *A Portrait of a Lady*,
the book he finished shortly before he died—
when he raised his eyes to me:
"Marcia— if I'd been born 100 years ago in Europe,
and someone— Tiresias, say— foretold the camps,
of what would happen to my children and grandchildren,
I cannot say that I would not have converted to Christianity."
'So says this putative descendant of Aaron,'
I thought as I left his den.

5.

1947, Irving,
the only year we had a tree
or that my mother made snow
after my father came home from the war,
the only time he gave Dan and me a Christmas present
or put together the words:
Marcia   Daniel   Christmas   1947   Love   Daddy.

According To the LA Times

"Even the stork in the sky knows her seasons/and the turtle dove swift, and the crane/keep the time of their coming/But my people pay no heed.../I planted you with noble vines/alas I find you changed into a base, an alien vine!" Jeremiah 8:7

Like you, I am filled with resentment, Jeremiah—
the words from the front page of the afternoon edition
of the December 7, 1963 Los Angeles Times
given me recently by my cousin: "H'wood Doctor found dead..."
"Distinguished physician...scribbled a note: 'everyone is innocent'...
plunged an 8-10 inch dissecting knife into his chest..."
(that he would have done it with his left hand, unsaid)—
under which lies an article entitled "Oswald Friend Talks."
What I want to know is:
    a) did he scribble before he plunged, or
    b) after; or, a skillful surgeon, did he
    c) dissect, as old rumor had it, a few layers
       of chest wall and then plunge? If b) or c), then
    d) how close had he come to his heart when he wrote
       "everyone is innocent," cutting the thread that
       spooled us to him?
    e) did his silence occur before or after Oswald's friend talked?
    f) finally, what is there to be learned from a newspaper
       using the words "scribbled" and "plunged"
       to speak of the death of my father?
          1. that there are no facts in words?
          2. that even Oswald had a friend?
          3. that everyone is neither guilty nor innocent?
          4. that all that is left me
             is a scimitar-shaped apostrophe,
             bringing forth a wilderness
             in which holy vines and
             holly vines intertwine,
             Jeremiah?

1976

Walking back from the park
to the new house, Emily and I—
a chilly afternoon in January,
having moved from Wisconsin six months ago
me, 34, newly remarried,
Emily, 5, shortly, she's been told,
to have a baby sister, says,
looking into the distance
as we come to an old arched wooden bridge,
"The sky was always blue in Madison,
wasn't it, Mommy?"

1942

They let my mother watch
the one in uniform take my hand to lead me away—
the backs of chubby legs,
hair cupped against the nape of my neck,
head tilted slightly toward him,
as if it were her father, she thinks,
guiding the child home
from a twilight walk along the seashore,
except that the ocean made no sound.

If I Hate My Husband

And if I hate my husband for growing old—
recoil from his shrinking,
from the confusion of hair—
as if time, ruing its work,
scrambled over the continents of the body
retrieving from groin and chest and armpits
more than could be held,
dropping willy-nilly like sheaves at dusk
on the innocent places: nostrils,
knuckles, toes—
spent and frightened of itself, crying
"I can take it back, take
it back, can
sweeten and smooth the rough and
bitter places," just
as I know
had I loved him more—
I would have stayed young for him
forever.

Provisioning

I have spent my life
laying up provisions
against disaster,
seeing only the clotting air
between what was said
and meant—
with each averted gaze,
closed hand,
assault, flood,
revolution,
I increased my stores—
and when someone came in want,
I gave only
what I needed least—
the gap they made
I repacked double,
until there is no more room
in my house,
and no one left
to preserve.

If the Universe

If the universe allowed our wheel
one backward turn,
what do you mourn—
what have I earned?
When a man I didn't know
whirled me on the dance floor
and I ascended like a star?
Or my father in his den,
hand fallen to his chest, a dying bird
beak lodged in his breast?
to release above,
or the wound below?
Transcendence or
death's sentence?
Or which is which?
I do not know.

The Solipsism Of the Suicide's Child

For a long time when I was a child
I thought I had cancer,
my stomach hurt so much,
but I was afraid to tell my father, the doctor,
thinking he would be mad at me—
And later, when for months and months
I was driven out of sleep by pinworms,
one morning early I heard him downstairs,
and in the milk-blue dawn I knelt across from him
as he read his AMA journal by the round coffee table
I'm writing at now—
Trying to form the words
I could not, for fear of his anger
and his disgust.
And when, at 50, my father took a seven-inch scalpel—
with which I knew he could have cured me if he had wanted,
cutting out quick and clean
my offending organs,
the bump on my nose— snip, snip—
and in the half-light of the new Sabbath, in his lab,
plunged it instead into his heart,
I could not tell of my grief
or relief
for now I knew
he was mad
at me.

For Primo Levi

Suffering becomes its own ground—
It is not that it cannot be borne,
But that we bear it too well—
To lie down on wooden planks
Stacked high like kindling,
Pressed for warmth against a sister bone bag,
We fall into a deep sleep,
Our bargain with God:
Dreams for agony—
All we had left
To keep us awake.

Steal Away

I like to steal things—
for example, today I tucked into my pocket
an almond bar from the food bank where I volunteer,
and often sneak into my neighbor's garden
when the flaming lilies bloom.
Yesterday I took the word *crumbling*
from someone else's poem,
waking this morning to secure it in my own,
knowing that if it doesn't come from my cupboard or garden
or womb,
if it breaks, or fades, or is lost,
I will not mind so much—
or if under the cover of night
it is spirited away
by someone like me.

At the Light

Stopped at the light on a gray winter morning

at Charleston and Middlefield

on my way back from Yonatan's school,

crossing the street, a young woman,

soft brown skin, smooth ponytail,

around her shoulders— not a jacket, but a blanket—

too cold   too poor, I look away,

look back   &

she's running down the street, hair swinging,

      tennis shoes white as doves

           blanket bluer than any sky.

Singing With Jennie

"You can't keep us girls down,"
our neighbor Jennie said
after our *how are you?*'s
as she opened the door to greet us,
and then "Oh honey, it's a dream to see you"—
"Alzheimer's" her husband had said
when we first stopped to chat last spring
and admire her garden,
"One has to call things by their name"—
"Alzheimer's" he said again to us this time,
having come to sing Christmas songs with Jennie,
a musician all her life—
today she's playing the piano, he's backing her up on the bass,
the four of us: one Methodist, one Presbyterian
and two Jews in January in California
singing "I'm Dreaming of a White Christmas"
once, twice, and then, again, once more,
until it is time to go, and she ushers us on our way,
calling from the corner, "Honey, it's a dream to see you,
just a dream."

Birthday Card

late afternoon—
oven door opening and closing,
refrigerator and cupboards too,
my husband's footsteps in the kitchen,
soft timpani of his preparations
as I lie down to wait for dinner
and read my book about the Supreme Court,
continuing the chapter on eminent domain and property rights—
when I see next to me on the pillow a card he has left—
I read the birthday message,
noting that he's misspelled *your*,
writing instead *you're*—
about to tell him gently, tactfully,
I change my mind so as not to embarrass him.
I'll carefully white-out the apostrophe and the 'e,'
imagine myself skillfully joining the 'u' and 'r,'
when he comes in, sees me holding the card,
points to his heart, "It came from here," he says
and walks back to the kitchen—
I reread slowly of his *devotion* and *joy*,
of my "understanding the space we need,"
his *to be* mine *to fly*
and I return the card to its place on the pillow,
having erased no mark Irving made,
or the space he intended between *you* and *are*,
the ground on which we often meet.

On Memory

The famous poet writes about forgetting
with a heartbreaking ending
that I will probably only remember inaccurately,
but whose haunting beauty, it seems,
belies its message:
"No wonder the moon in the window
seems to have drifted/out of a love poem
that you used to know by heart."
But I wonder, is it really so terrible to forget—
that "the author's name has fled" &
"the quadratic equation"
(which to be honest, I never knew in the first place)
perhaps this is as it should be:
our memories migrating, setting up shop with our children,
others we love—
Isn't clutching at memories
its own sort of avarice—
another kind of greed?
That all the names of all the books and all the wars
stitch us to a fading landscape
of paper and print—
Perhaps it is not the naming of objects that binds us together
but the asking, "Emily,
what did I used to tell you
that drove you crazy
and now you say to your children?"
and her laughing response:
"I know you can figure it out."
"Claire, remember the scary story
about the grandmother and the murderer—
who wrote that again?"
and her gentle reminder: "Flannery."
Had I remembered,
I would not need their gifts
nor they mine—

continued...

like what appeared to my mother
the night before she died,
after 10 days of reading to her
the poets she loved, and had read to me
since I was young: Auden and Dickinson,
Ransom, Williams, and Yeats,
when in the watercolor on the wall opposite where she lay—
the artist she no longer remembered—
her old friend, Florence Schull, whose apartment she rented
on the Ponte Vecchio in 1967, the flood year
or that she had written a startlingly beautiful journal— now lost—
of those days, or even that this was a sea shell—
what she saw instead, rapt at its turnings,
her last words to me: "Look, Marcia, see—
a baby hiding there."

And when my time comes to die,
if all that drifts back to me
is that shell waiting
beneath a moon, blue
as in the corny song
I loved when I was 16,
I think it will be enough
to see me through.

Spring

Letter From London In 1958 When I Was Sixteen

      from My Father

Dearest Marcia,
I have just come from seeing Margot Fonteyn
in Ondine— wonderful in every sense of the word—
the whole first act she hardly seemed to touch the ground or have a
bone in her body,
the second was like a Greek tragedy in pantomime,
the third filled with folk, acrobatic, and almost modern— great fun,
tho' I saw it all alone [the *all* added with a caret].
Then intermission and a burst of applause:
everyone on the main floor turned to look at the box
above where I was sitting, the news spread through the audience:
"The Queen Mother is in attendance."
At the next intermission I slipped around to the other side
to get a glimpse of her—
She was very queenly, dressed in pink and pretty,
even tho' quite chubby. At the end of the performance
some people lined the narrow street at the exit of her box—
Pretty soon, down the steps you could see her come,
first a pink slipper, moving ever so slowly downward—
then, gradually, the Queen!
She slowly entered her black limousine
and turned to smile— everyone clapped
and I waved my rolled up program.
Then she waved back [he was so handsome then].
We all waved and clapped and she drove off,
followed by another black limousine whom we applauded, as well,
and, right after, along came some college kids
in a little old red jalopy, who were cheered and applauded even more,
then everyone left for home quite happy

                                                       continued...

[he not home, but to his hotel]—
I am sending you a program that a queen waved at.
Don't study too hard— just enough to get a modest card
of straight A's—
(you know of course that I am joking, and yet
am being just a tiny bit serious.)
Love, Dad.

Joseph Le Conte Junior High School

6 blocks east and
8 blocks south of Hollywood & Vine
"Joseph Le Conte, Savant and Scientist,"
carved into the pediment
above the stone columns,
fixed too,
I'm just landed from Minneapolis
frozen, scared, and
sorrowfully plain,
stunned on a cement bench
with three other new girls,
they're swaying, chanting
and on one a name tag swings,
"Nona Privateer"
  (no doubloons
   peg leg
   parrot)
but hair so precisely arranged, and still,
marmoreal thicket of that wondrous Pachuco headdress—
they sing, harmonizing
the only words in any language
that even now, my throat closes around:

> *tough titty, says the kitty*
> *but the milk's still good;*
> *tough titty, says the kitty*
> *but the milk's still good.*

remembering only now, at this writing,
my old name, Marci Katz, teased to Kitty Katz.
So I hung around instead with Cathy Mace, Shelly Patterson,

continued...

Judy Nestor, and Susie Hymowitz
(who by the age of 16 had read
all of Mortimer Adler's Great Books)
and their queen, goddess and
Chief Druidess, Becky Leigh
        whose beguiling lisp
            caused a lingual plague of such proportions
            that teams of speech therapists
            had to be airlifted in—
to give her her due,
it was Becky who gave me the only
useful piece of information I acquired in junior high school
where each morning
in the huge stone bathroom
at the bottom of the administration building,
I saw her tiny fingers, nimble as butterflies
at the waist of her bright blouse
when two perfect pleats appeared
swelling the soft cotton
just exactly where her breasts
should have been—

Becky Leigh
whose flesh, utterly juiced, congealed
and became plastic in 1959
and Barbie is born
and the new phenomenon
confirms the old theology, slightly recast:
the inheritance of the sins
of the mothers—
Listen up, Becky Leigh:
evolution never has been
a one-way street.
And she married her first love,
Ricky Lyme, the most popular boy at Hollywood High School—

and its student body president—
soon to become the very well known, and articulate, young minister
of the Hollywood First Presbyterian Church
on Franklin and Cahuenga,
the Protestant church with the largest congregation
and skating rink in Southern California
where on my fourteenth birthday, on March 14th,
Bobbie Grumbles skates next to me,
easing his left foot in front of mine,
tripping me so I can't leave him,
even for my family's party—
arriving finally home at 10 o'clock
to no party, no dinner, a $5 bill and a note: "It's late. go to bed."
on the dining room table.

The day after that, my arm in a cast,
Bobbie Grumbles, 5 feet, 11 inches in 9th grade,
soft blond crew-cut
low slung jeans
and white T-shirt
walks me home down Franklin Avenue,
holding his brown leather jacket out,
like wings—
pointing to cars with delicate pin striped designs,
"Von Dutching," he told me, the artist's name—
       more intricate than Dürer
           more soaring than Blake—
cars appearing everywhere—Gramercy, Cheremoya, Franklin
   down Wilton, down Fountain, and Taft—
       like illuminated manuscripts
           floating
   toward Hollywood & Vine.
But as I knew it had to happen
the next Wednesday Bobbie Grumbles skated away
with Cathy Mace

continued...

whose boobs were so big
she made off
with anything she ever wanted—
Coyote, Trickster,
she smoked
she cheated
she snuck into every movie theater
on Hollywood Boulevard,
she made out everywhere
and anywhere
and became the youngest principal in the history
of the Los Angeles school system,
for her mother was a principal
and primogeniture will out.

Then at the end of a long school day
at the end of a gray November in 1974
when she was 30,
Cathy Mace lay down on her living room couch
and a tiny tube
no bigger than a thread
sprang a tiny leak
in her head
and shortly thereafter she died.
But last year I found out that Bobbie Grumbles
is a successful real estate developer
in Orange County,
leaving open still
the question of comeuppance.
But years and years before
on a warm spring morning,
cruelly unbudded
and so left to my own sly devices,
positioned inside my beginner's bra
two satiny falsies—
and at Joseph Le Conte Junior High School,

as PE drifts into algebra,
algebra into lunch, and I,
blissfully unaware of their secret shifting,
slipping toward the arm hole
of my sleeveless cotton blouse,
one appears to Gerry Fusco,
who tells Cathy Mace—
I made her tell him that wasn't what he saw,
because she owed me—
she told me she swore to him
that she knew I owned no such things,
that couldn't have been what he saw,
it must have been a part of my strapless peeking through,
she said—
and I close my eyes this instant
to see him wink.

O the seaweed sheen of Gerry Fusco's hair—
its amphibious gleam.

The Chemistry Of Love

Now that my children have all left home
and I'm retired on a modest pension,
my relationship with my clothes has altered, so to speak,
grown more close-knit—
No longer do I carelessly toss them on the bookcase next to my bed
to lie in a heap, crumpled one on top of the other, for days on end,
knowing there's plenty more where they came from,
Nordstrom, a hop, skip, and a jump away
and my resources generally adequate
to my students' finely-honed sensitivity to diversity
of a sartorial kind—
Instead, these days when I remove, for example, a sweater,
no matter how tired I am, I lay it gently on my bed,
smoothing the creases, patting away the furrows,
and with the tips of my fingers, take a sleeve,
placing it lightly across the torso, then the other
to rest snugly across its mate,
finally I fold the sweater carefully, yoga-like at the waist,
and carry it to my closet,
where it will lie in the cool depths of my trundled chest—
loosened threads tightening, torn fibers mending,
molecules duplicating, as atoms of carbon and oxygen,
hydrogen, sulfur and nitrogen array themselves in perfect symmetry,
repairing the delicate tracery of branching filaments,
cells rehydrating, plumping, colors deepening in the dark silence—
restoring itself for me as it waits in solemn anticipation
of just the right moment when I will lift it tenderly
to unfurl like a spring flower, radiant in its promise
that never will I need ever buy anything
to clothe me again.

At the Bank With Claire 30 Years Ago

"That's a good way to learn about death,"
the white haired woman in the bank said to me
(about giving children goldfish: "They frequently die,"
I had just said to her, holding Claire
by the fish tank we were admiring in the B of A)—
"Claire's older sister had so many things die,
two guinea pigs, one right after the other"—
the second one I held all night, gurgling with tuberculosis,
pink foam on my sleeve—
"She wants a cat," I said,
"but our street is so busy. I know it will get away."
"Very likely, my dear, very likely—
and that would be a trauma. My daughter—
she's almost 50 now— when she was three months old,
we set her on a pallet by the goldfish bowl,
she'd heave her head up and up 'til it shook,
and she'd just watch and watch."
"They love the movement and color," I said.
"Oh yes— but the life," she murmured.
"The motion," I added.
"The life," she said.

A True Story

Babysitting at my daughter's house,
early morning coffee warming me,
waiting for Mika and Yonatan to wake,
I take a cereal box from the shelf—
Gorilla Crunch— and read the back
about Kareba, a young mountain gorilla,
two months older than my grandson,
who was born 18 days shy of 2000,
just missing messianic status (though his mother would disagree)—
Kareba, too, when ignored, starts to whimper,
the longer his mother's absence, the louder the wails—
soon he's pounding the ground and pulling up plants,
until finally she comes back, holds him and grooms him,
and I think 'What a good mother gorilla
Emily would make,'
and, so, to reward her, I begin tidying her room
where I see, lying on the bookshelf next to her bed,
neatly folded, a banana peel.

Philip

Philip, our ten-year-old grandson

thinks a lot about things:

"Discipline," he says,

"I've been thinking about that—

My teacher told Tori

in front of the whole class

that if she didn't hurry up

she could finish her work

in the kindergarten room.

But I would give people rewards

for doing their work, like

playing Nintendo.

That's what I'm going to do

if I'm a principal.

I think that's better

than making people feel

ashamed."

Reading Borges

Sitting in bed against a plumped up pillow,
I'm mending my grandson's slacks
while my husband reads aloud a Borges story
about a universe composed entirely of hexagons,
infinite in number, in an infinitely large room, "The Library,"
filled with soaring spiral stairways,
immense shelves of books whose meaning is indecipherable,
as is at first this story to me—
but as I sew, slowly, painstakingly,
stitch by tiny stitch,
I hem myself into a world of endless hexagons,
of glowing spherical fruit reflected in countless polished mirrors
and a continuous book he calls 'God'
and I think of the cloud-enveloped Yahweh,
Zeus, the Shape-Shifter,
of all the warnings against encroaching upon the gods,
of Amos and Tiresias and Hosea,
the fate of Moses and Lear, alone, at the very end, in the wilderness,
of Lucifer, who outshone the rest,
of Niobe, and Medusa, and Arachne,
she who wove a cloth blue as the heavens,
and again I'm leaning against my mother's knees
as she brushes my hair
and reads to me *Alice in Wonderland*,
having come to the last page
where Alice, exceeding her limits (as all traitors do),
swells to towering size,
bears down on the shrinking monarchs—
"Who cares for you?" she scoffs,
"You're nothing but a pack of cards!"
as I finish my last stitch, turn to my husband now fast asleep,
then back to Yonatan's slacks,
make a knot, and cut the thread.

Violation

"I made a rolling stop today,"

I'd tell the cop from Menlo Park,

"So smooth, so slow,

it felt so good—"

"I know just what you mean," he'd say,

"Like the arabesque of bullet

coursing to the flesh—

the salutation, pulse, and cry,

then the spasm deep inside."

Karen

I didn't see my 17-year-old student
the year she was being treated
for cancer of the spine.
I didn't see her before or after the surgery
that nicked her backbone.
or the two bouts of radiation.
or the two doses of chemotherapy.
But before the last and final dose
she called to have coffee
and give me three college rec forms.
When we were finished I asked if I could keep her company
as she checked herself in that morning.

Driving behind her, I stop when she stops,
see her hand reach out quickly,
purposefully, her arm curved
    Not like a reed
    Not like a Japanese brush stroke
    Not like Pavlova's
but poised for an instant
in perfect stillness—
until before my eyes can see,
the ticket, her arm, her hand
have all disappeared,
and the black car is moving on
toward the waiting hospital.

Yeats Changes His Itinerary

There is a forest in Thailand
where white-handed gibbons live
and sing of danger
and to find a mate—
then paired for life they croon duets,
notes rearranging as the old wood shifts,
as the foliage dips and rises,
and their neighbors sing back.   Yeats
wanted out of time, release
from 'the sensual music of dying generations,'
to be a bird of gold rousing an emperor from sleep,
but I think— if only he'd subscribed to Science News,
read the issue for last January 6,
he might have said:
"On second thought, Byzantium can wait,
and let the emperor dream in peace tonight—
I'm on my way to the Khao Lai Forest
to hear the gibbons sing."

"Joe Hill"

As my husband sings to our grandson,
his sweet, sad *shtetl* baritone
turning even "the wheels on the bus go round and round"
into a lament, I think, 'Take heart, my dear,
I'm falling in love with you all over again,'
remembering our drive to Santa Barbara,
the first time we ever sang together:
"The Four Insurgent Generals," "The Peat-Bog Soldiers,"
"Skye Boat Song," "Joe Hill"—
and when in the promise of "I never died, said he,"
I became yours, who would deny 'Eternal Return,'
when now, 30 years later, singing to Yonatan as we walk,
Joe rounds the corner in his bus,
union man still—
hailing us as we cross to the park
where we keep on singing,
and Yonatan swings back and forth, back
and forth, back and forth.

Notes

If Voices. *Kine hora* is Yiddish for 'May there not be an evil eye.'

Gentle Annie. "Pilgrim soul" is an allusion to a line in the Yeats poem, "When You Are Old."

Christmas, 1947. *Meshuggah* is Yiddish for 'crazy.'

On Memory. The quoted lines in the beginning of the poem are from the Billy Collins poem, "Forgetfulness." The last two lines are an homage to Lorine Niedecker's poem, "My Little Granite Pail."

Yeats Changes His Itinerary. The quoted lines are from the Yeats poem, "Sailing to Byzantium."

"Joe Hill." *Shtetl* is a Yiddish word for a pre-World War II small town or village in Eastern Europe with a large Jewish population.

"Joe Hill." 'Eternal Return' is a philosophical idea attributed to Nietzsche, among others, claiming that because matter is finite and time infinite, everything that exists recurs.

About the Author

The Grandmother Poems is Marcia Katz Wolf's third collection of poetry. The first, *River, Rivers*, was published in 1996; the second, *Inheritance*, in 2006. She was a music therapist for several years, and then a teacher, having retired three years ago to spend more time with her family and on her writing. She lives with her husband in Palo Alto.